THE PLEASURES OF COUNTRY SPORTS

A Pavilion Companion

Introduction

Man's natural instincts for hunting have been carefully refined through the ages. The necessity of gaining food for survival, although still fervently carried out by peasant and poacher, first developed in medieval times into courtly sport, as enthusiastic kings, the richest landowners, conducted their affairs, both state and private, on the hunting field.

Their courtiers expanded this tradition, and through practising field sports on their extensive estates, widened their circle of influence by impressing others not only with the wealth of their game and land, but with accompanying feasts and festivities, thereby setting a standard that became "de rigeur": a gentleman was not a gentleman unless he also enjoyed hunting, shooting or fishing, and preferably all three.

This developed in the grand manner throughout the eighteenth century, as father taught son the skills of these sports. Thus by the nineteenth century, a tradition of the country house party had been established. Whereas before, horse transport somewhat limited travel, now the Industrial Revolution and the coming of the railways meant everyone who was anyone could go to Scotland in pursuit of the teeming game, whether to stand in line with rifle or walk for miles in pursuit of elusive stags, or gaze contemplatively on a riverbank, waiting for salmon to bite.

The ladies would entertain themselves, ensuring light entertainment at mealtimes. Baronial style shooting lodges abounded, and specific dates for the opening and closing of the season for shooting certain birds established. The best fishing for salmon has always been in Scotland or Ireland, but further south in England the trout rivers hold as much attraction for the keen fisherman.

Riding to hounds with a fox as quarry has now become a contentious issue with anti-field sports protesters (mainly urban) objecting to the pastimes of the hunting classes on the grounds of animal

rights. But to a farmer a fox steals animals, thus the law of the jungle prevails. As a certain snob cachet developed, raising certain hunts above the rest in terms of superiority – the Beaufort, Heythrop, Quorn and Pytchley being amongst the front rank – so Oscar Wilde was inspired to the infamous comment that hunting was nothing but "the unspeakable in pursuit of the uneatable". Still it seems that country people cannot be distracted from the pleasure of riding out on clear mornings over open country, with the thrill of the chase and a good day's riding with friends as their main objective.

This small volume celebrates these pleasures from the mid-nineteenth to twentieth centuries, with the warmth and spirit in which they were indulged.

Jenny de Gex, 1991

HUNTING

Hunting is a game for princes and noble persons; it hath been highly prized in all ages; it was one of the qualifications that Xenophon bestowed on his Cyrus, that he was a hunter of wild beasts. Hunting trains up the younger nobility to the use of manly exercises in their riper age. What more manly exercise than hunting the wild boar, the stag, the buck, the fox, or the hare? How doth it preserve health, and increase strength and activity!

The Compleat Angler, Izaak Walton, 1653

For Shooting and Hunting Visits

The amount of clothes taken for a shooting or a hunting visit depends entirely upon its length.

The amount taken for a week-end visit is, however, a safe basis to work upon outside the special kit necessary for shooting or riding. When the visit is for several days it is always wiser to take an extra shirt or two, socks, collars, and handkerchiefs, in case of accident. For such a visit it is wise also to include the evening tail-coat and white waistcoat, in case there is a dance or a big dinner-party at the house in which one is staying.

The Book of Etiquette, Lady Troubridge, 1926

Kitting Out

Let us now suppose him breakfasted, and ready for a start.

He was 'got up' with uncommon care in the most complete style of the severe order of sporting costume. It being now the commencement of the legitimate hunting season – the first week in November – he availed himself of the privileged period for turning out in everything new. Rejecting the now generally worn cap, he adhered to the heavy, close-napped hat, described in our opening chapter, whose connexion with his head, or back, if it came off, was secured by a small black silk cord, hooked through the band by a fox's tooth, and anchored to a button inside the haven of his low coat-collar. His neck was enveloped in the ample folds of a large white silk cravat, tied in a pointing diamond tie, and secured with a large silver horse-shoe pin, the shoe being almost large enough for the foot of a young donkey.

His low, narrow-collared coat was of the infinitesimal order; that is to say, a coat, and yet as little of a coat as possible – very near a jacket, in fact. The seams, of course, were outside, and were it not for the extreme strength and evenness of the sewing and the evident intention of the thing, an ignorant person might have supposed that he had had his coat turned. A double layer of cloth extended the full length of the outside of the sleeves, much in the fashion of the stage-coachmen's greatcoats in former times; and instead of cuffs, the sleeves were carried out to the ends of the fingers, leaving it to the fancy of the wearer to sport a long cuff or a short cuff, or no cuff at all – just as the weather dictated. Though the coat was single-breasted, he had a hole made on the button side, to enable him to keep it together by means of a miniature snaffle, instead of a button. The snaffle passed across his chest, from whence the coatee, flowing easily back, displayed the broad ridge and furrow of a white cord waistcoat, with a low step collar . . .

Mr Sponge's Sporting Tour, R.S. Surtees, 1853

The Meet

We trotted to the meet together. My companion was calm, and very pretty. I judged her to be a schoolgirl of about sixteen; that she did not hunt regularly, by the cut of her boots, which were too large round the calves. Her dark breeches, too, looked ready-made. I rammed my hat on the back of my head, feeling myself a reg'lar top-sawyer over the timber – until I remembered the shaggy ungroomed coat and long sweeping tail under me. I set my hat at a more sedate angle.

Hounds were grouped against an old barn wall of weathered oak and brick. Brown collars to the pink uniforms, the usual lean small huntsman with red hacksaw features and marvellous polish of thin boots, sitting as though he had grown into his horse. Apparently the girl knew none of the faces. She sat quietly there, composed, aloof but not shy, looking around with frank eyes. Anxious lest she should think I was trying to make an impression on her, which I admitted to myself I was trying to do, I remained aloof yet alert near her, but neither looking at her directly nor speaking to her. A tall woman on foot in a grey coat and skirt, and carrying a blackthorn thumb-stick, moved among the horses and stood by the grey's head. "Hullo, Annabelle, it's a big field, isn't it? How's The Learned Pig behaving?"

"I like him, Mummie. Where's Queenie?"

"She's with the General." The newcomer and I exchanged glances. I began a search for my cigarette case, in the flap of my new yellow waistcoat.

We moved off. A fox was found in the middle of a ploughed field, in a slight depression. The chestnut was quickly wet with sweat. When put to a big thorn fence, it refused to jump, to my relief. Soon I was one of a straggling cavalcade seeking gaps and gateways.

The Sun in the Sands, Henry Williamson, 1945

Ladies in the Field

Still, there are many ways that young ladies may insinuate themselves into the good graces of sportsmen without following them into the hunting-field. Talking about their horses, above all admiring them, taking an interest in their sport, seeing that they have nice papers of sandwiches to take out with them, or recommending them to be bled when they came home with dirty faces after falls.

'And do *you* like horses?' asked his lordship, darting sharply round on Emily, who had been yielding, or rather submitting to the precedence of her sister.

'Oh yes; and hounds too!' replied she eagerly.

'And hounds, too!' exclaimed his lordship, with a start, and another hearty bang of the fist, adding, 'well, now, I like a woman that likes hounds.'

Mr Sponge's Sporting Tour, R.S. Surtees, 1853

The Great Run

A quarter of a mile or so this way were a couple of dots of horsemen, one on a white, the other on a dark colour – most likely Jones, the keeper, and Farmer Stubble, on the foaly mare. Then, a little nearer, was a man in a hedge, trying to coax his horse after him, stopping the way of two boys in white trousers, whose ponies looked like rats. Again, a little nearer, were some of the persevering ones – men who still hold on in the forlorn hopes of a check – all dark-coated, and mostly trousered. Then came the last of the red-coats – Tom Washball, Charley Joyce, and Sam Sloman, riding well in the first flight of second horsemen – his lordship's pad-groom, Mr Fossick's man in drab with a green collar, Mr Wake's in blue, also a lad in scarlet and a flat hat, with a second horse for the huntsman. Drawing still nearer came the ruck – men in red, men in brown, men in livery, a farmer or two in fustian, all mingled together; and a few hundred yards before these, and close upon his lordship, were the *élite* of the field – five men in scarlet and one in black.

Mr Sponge's Sporting Tour, R.S. Surtees, 1853

Reynard the Fox

The hounds and the hunt were limping home;
Limping home in the dark dead-beaten,
The hounds all rank from a fox they'd eaten.
Dansey saying to Robin Dawe:
"The fastest and longest I ever saw."
And Robin answered: "Oh, Tom, 'twas good!
I thought they'd changed in the Mourne End Wood,
But now I feel that they did not change.
We've had a run that was great and strange;
And to kill in the end, at dusk, on grass!
We'll turn to the Cock and take a glass,
For the hounds, poor souls! are past their forces;
And a gallon of ale for our poor horses,
And some bits of bread for the hounds, poor things!
After all they've done (for they've done like kings),
Would keep them going till we get in.
We had it alone from Nun's Wood Whin."

Reynard the Fox, John Masefield, 1923

SHOOTING

The words which Lord Warwick wrote at the beginning of his autobiography could easily have been written by King Edward: 'I have carried out my official duties as long and as faithfully as I can, and for the rest I have lived in such fashion as seemed most agreeable to me . . . convinced that a good day's shooting is second in point of pleasure to nothing else on earth.' What Edward pioneered at Sandringham, was followed on numerous other estates. We can follow the King on his tour of them – Merton, Holkham and Quidenham in Norfolk, and further afield, Elveden, West Dean, Crichel, Castle Rising, Hall Barn, Welbeck and a score of others.

The Big Shots, J.G. Ruffer, 1977

Big Shots

"That's all the story," he went on. "I don't like the man myself, but he is a wonderful pheasant shot, which passes him everywhere. Shooting has become a kind of fetish in these parts, Mr Quartermain. For instance, it is a tradition on this estate that we must kill more pheasants than on any other in the county, and therefore I have to ask the best guns, who are not always the best fellows. It annoys me, but it seems that I must do what was done before me."

"Under those circumstances I should be inclined to give up the thing altogether, Lord Ragnall. Sport as sport is good, but when it becomes a business it grows hateful. I know, who have had to follow it as a trade for many years."

The Ivory Child, H. Rider Haggard, 1916

Men and their Guns

A man who is going to shoot must provide his own cartridges. He is not expected to bring a loader other than his own valet, who will act in that capacity. A loader is provided by the host for a man who does not bring a valet.

A loader is not needed unless a man uses two guns. A man is expected to have a pair of guns if he accepts an invitation to a large shoot.

The Book of Etiquette, Lady Troubridge, 1926

The Shooting Season

The shooting season opens on 12th August with grouse-shooting in Scotland and the North of England.

Partridge shooting begins on 1st September and ends on 1st February.

Pheasant shooting begins on 1st October and ends on 1st February.

Hares may be shot up to 1st March. Rabbits can be shot all the year round; rooks in the spring.

The Book of Etiquette, Lady Troubridge, 1926

Points of Shooting Etiquette

By the 1890s, the men's shooting dress had become standardised. Tailcoats and waistcoats, once the outfit of every shooting man, were still to be seen on many of the estate's keepers but the more useful Harris Tweed shooting suits had replaced them among the guns. Each shooting man would have these made by his own tailor, to his own specifications, and so there was still plenty of variety to be seen on a shooting field. The royal family, and particularly the Prince of Wales (King George V) wore shooting spats, and these were quickly taken up by others, including Lord de Grey and the Duleep Singhs.

Only a certain latitude was allowed on the shooting field, however, and eccentricity was frowned upon. Lord Rossmore fancied a pair of jodhpurs which were popularised by the Duke of Connaught when he came back from India. Rossmore had some made in black buckskin, and he was so pleased with the way they looked that he wore them out shooting at Elveden. When King Edward VII spied them, he came over and said, 'I'm glad to see, Rossmore, that you are using up your old evening trousers to make shooting leggings.' His hat, too, came in for a similar badinage. General Strachey, who was also shooting at Elveden said of it 'By jove! I am not a wealthy man, but I would willingly give £1,000 to have the impertinent audacity to wear that hat.' Lord Suffield was also renowned for the eccentricity of his hats. One, which he wore at Sandringham, was described as 'incredibly awful, looking as if it had been fashioned by a pickaxe and shovel and rolled over by a dozen or more buses.'

The Big Shots, J.G. Ruffer, 1977

THE INEVITABLE PHOTOGRAPH

The shooting houseparties at Blenheim had by the 1890s become as splendid and influential as at Chatsworth. In 1896 the Prince of Wales expressed a wish to come to shoot there and his arrival for a shooting party in the autumn of that year marked a social high point at Blenheim. Many of the political leaders of the time were there: Arthur Balfour, later Prime Minister, wrote of the week: 'There is here a big party in a big house in a big park beside a big lake. To begin with (as our Toast lists have it) "the Prince of Wales" and the rest of the Royal Family –' or if not quite that, at least a quorum, namely himself, his wife, two daughters and a son-in-law. There are two sets of George Curzons, the Londonderrys, Grenfells, Gosfords, H. Chaplin, etc., etc. We came down by special train – rather cross most of us – were received with illuminations, guards of honour, cheering and other follies, went through agonies about our luggage, but finally settled down placidly enough.

'Today the men shot and the women dawdled. As I detest both occupations equally, I stayed in my room until one o'clock and then went exploring on my bike, joining everybody at luncheon. Then, after the inevitable photograph, I again betook myself to my faithful machine and here I am writing to you. So far you perceive the duties of society are weighing lightly upon me.'

The Big Shots, J.G. Ruffer, 1977

Mr Jorrocks in Trouble

Suddenly his reverie was interrupted by the discharge of a gun in the field adjoining the hedge along which he was passing, and the boisterous *whirring* of a great cock-pheasant over his head, which caused his horse to start and stop short, and to nearly pitch Jorrocks over his head. The bird was missed, but the sportsman's dog dashed after it, with all the eagerness of expectation, regardless of the cracks of the whip – the 'comes to heel,' and 'downs to charge' of the master. Jorrocks pulled out his hunting telescope, and having marked the bird down with the precision of a billiard-table keeper, rode to the gate to acquaint the shooter with the fact, when to his infinite amazement he discovered his friend, Nosey Browne (late of 'The Surrey'), who since his affairs had taken the unfortunate turn mentioned in our last paper, had given up hunting and determined to confine himself to shooting only. Nosey, however, was no great performer, as may be inferred, when we say that he had been in pursuit of the above-mentioned cock-pheasant ever since day-break, and after firing thirteen shots at him had not yet touched a feather.

Jorrocks Jaunts and Jollities, R.S. Surtees, 1874

STALKING

"Without doubt deer-stalking is one of the most fatiguing, but it is also one of the most interesting of pursuits. There is not a tree, or a bush behind which you can hide yourself … One has, therefore, to be constantly on the alert in order to circumvent them; and to keep under the hill out of their wind, crawling on hands and knees, and dressed entirely in grey."

Leaves From a Journal of Our Life in the Highlands,

Queen Victoria, 1868

LEFT LUGGAGE
ROOMS

To Glen Fishie and Grantown

Then we came upon a most lovely spot – the scene of all Landseer's glory – and where there is a little encampment of wooden and turf huts, built by the late Duchess of Bedford; now no longer belonging to the family and, alas! all falling into decay – among splendid fir-trees, the mountains rising abruptly from the sides of the valley. We were quite enchanted with the beauty of the view. This place is about seven miles from the mouth of the *Fishie*. Emerging from the wood we came upon a good road, with low hills, beautifully heather-coloured, to the left; those to the right, high and wooded, with noble corries and waterfalls.

Leaves From a Journal of Our Life in the Highlands, Queen Victoria, 1868

A Stag at Bay

After luncheon, Albert decided to walk through the wood for the last time, to have a last chance, and allowed Vicky and me to go with him. At half-past three o'clock we started, got out at Grant's, and walked up part of *Carrop*, intending to go along the upper path, when a stag was heard to roar, and we all turned into the wood. We crept along, and got into the middle path. Albert soon left us to go lower, and we sat down to wait for him; presently we heard a shot – then complete silence – and, after another pause of some little time, three more shots. This was again succeeded by complete silence. We sent some one to look, who shortly returned, saying the stag had been twice hit and they were after him. Macdonald next went, and in about five minutes we heard "Solomon" give tongue, and knew he had the stag at bay.

Leaves From a Journal of Our Life in the Highlands, Queen Victoria, 1868

Stalking Hints

1. Spy carefully all ground.
2. Make a mental note of all deer.
3. Select a prominent mark about all deer which can be recognised from other positions so as to locate the deer.
4. Keep close together during the stalk and do what the stalker does when and where he does it.
5. If part of the stalk is to be in sight of the deer, choose the alternative route (if any) where movement in sight is at the maximum distance from the deer.
6. Never hurry except in very special circumstances.
7. Take plenty of cartridges (15-20). Things can go wrong e.g. if the telescope sight gets knocked.
8. Carry a compass, whistle, crepe bandage (for sprained ankles, and a small roll of sticking plaster (useful for repairing many things as well as you!) as a minimum first aid.

Deer Stalking, Edmund Luxmoore, 1980

FISHING

O sir, doubt not that angling is an art. Is it not an art to deceive a trout with an artificial fly? a trout! that is more sharp-sighted than any hawk you have named, and more watchful and timorous than your high-mettled merlin is bold; and yet I doubt not to catch a brace or two to-morrow for a friend's breakfast: doubt not, therefore, sir, but that angling is an art, and an art worth your learning.

The Compleat Angler, Izaak Walton, 1653

His First Trout

Here's the catch of the season. Behold and
take heed,
Ye benders of greenheart on Tayside and Tweed,
All ye who have tempted with minnow or fly
Her treasure from Leven, her wealth from the Wye!
Before us stand silent, all ye who would boast
Of tarpons ye fought on the Florida coast,
Of strong-running rainbows that fell to your hook
Where the tawny snow-water comes down from
Mount Cook,
Of the baskets the swift-trotting bronchos brought
home
From the canyon where pools of the White River
foam!

Your thirty-pound salmon sent ne'er such a thrill
Through the proud man that played him by
Rutherford Mill
As is throbbing this moment right home to the
heart
Of the tiniest angler from Tummel to Dart.
Your seven-pound trout had no power as a prize
To kindle such light in his conqueror's eyes
As is lit in the deeps of those blue ones that gaze
On 'the trout that *I* catched' on this day of all days.
No gold can out-glory, no jewel surpass
This atom of silver that gleams in the grass.

The Collected Sporting Verse of Will H. Ogilvie, 1932

How Big is your Fish?

I am not a good fisherman myself. I devoted a considerable amount of attention to the subject at one time, and was getting on, as I thought, fairly well; but the old hands told me that I should never be any real good at it, and advised me to give it up. They said that I was an extremely neat thrower, and that I seemed to have plenty of gumption for the thing, and quite enough constitutional laziness. But they were sure I should never make anything of a fisherman. I had not got sufficient imagination.

They said that as a poet, or a shilling shocker, or a reporter, or anything of that kind, I might be satisfactory, but that, to gain any position as a Thames angler, would require more play of fancy, more power of invention than I appeared to possess. Some people are under the impression that all that is required to make a good fisherman is the ability to tell lies easily and without blushing; but this is a mistake. Mere bald fabrication is useless; the veriest tyro can manage that. It is in the circumstantial detail, the embellishing touches of probability, the general air of scrupulous – almost of pedantic – veracity, that the experienced angler is seen.

Anybody can come in and say, "Oh, I caught fifteen dozen perch yesterday evening"; or "Last Monday I landed a gudgeon, weighing eighteen pounds, and measuring three feet from the tip to the tail."

Three Men In A Boat, Jerome K. Jerome, 1889

Spring Salmon

The greatest of all sport in fly-fishing is that for spring salmon in a big river. It is in kind quite different from fly-fishing for trout. It is only by courtesy that the arrangement of feathers, especially on the huge hooks used in early spring, can be called a fly; and the motion of the fly in the water, carried round by the stream at the end of a long tight line, has no resemblance to that of any known insect; the fly works sunk in the water, and in spring is generally taken by the salmon without any break or sign on the surface of the river. What the angler expects is not a visible rise, but a sudden tightening of the line by a strong and undeniable pull. The sensation of this pull, especially if it comes after an hour or more of casting and unfulfilled expectation, is one of the great moments in the joy of life; if the salmon be well hooked, it is followed by a period – it may be anything from five minutes to half an hour – of intense anxiety and strain, to be consummated, if all ends well, by a feeling of triumph and admiration, when the splendid beauty of a fresh-run salmon is contemplated on the bank.

Fallodon Papers, Viscount Grey of Fallodon, 1926

Irish Waters

Salmon Pool was the first on the way down that I fished. It is an irregularly shaped piece of water, wide spreading at the top and well timbered on both sides of the bank. The fish lie close to the east side, and I commenced operations about half-way down, paying special attention to the locality of the big rock over which the water was breaking and forming a tempting looking eddy. It was just the spot in a swift river where a fish would be likely to rest, and the Spiddal rushes at express speed for the greater part of its journey to the sea. If I were without a guide on a strange river, it is the place where I should expect a fish to give me a tight line. The water was breaking round the rock with great violence, and possibly made too swift a current for a comfortable resting-place. Were the water six inches lower the conditions would have been more favourable.

The Angler's Guide to the Irish Fisheries, Joseph Adams, 1924

The Art of Dapping

There is an interval, however, between the appearance of the trout and the submersion of the fly. The whole art of dapping lies in the way the angler behaves himself during the interval. What is more natural than to strike the moment the break is seen in the water? What is more difficult than to refrain for one second of time from striking? Habits become second nature, and the involuntary muscular action will take place despite all vows and promises made to the contrary. One may pledge himself, but he cannot pledge ganglionic centres. Afferent and efferent nerves will come into play, and one's will unconsciously becomes commander and chief in the act of betrayal. How well we know this in shooting! Up goes the gun, and the trigger is pressed. It is somebody else's bird, or a young pheasant before the First of October, but the action had got so far under way that there is no crying off, and the next moment – we'll leave that, please. The first hold a trout takes of the daddy is by the legs and wings, which bulk largest in his physiognomy. To strike immediately, means a division of the spoil, the fish sharing in one part of the fly and the angler in the other. The moment the daddy is dragged under the trout takes a firmer grip, which generally includes the hook; a strike then is followed by resistance. The great thing is not to strike until the daddy disappears. The angler who can harden himself to such a self-denying ordinance will undoubtedly give the best account of himself at the close of the day.

The Angler's Guide to the Irish Fisheries, Joseph Adams, 1924

A Day's Dry-fly-fishing

Let a sample of a day's dry-fly-fishing on a chalk stream in the latter half of May be taken first. The angler is by the river not later than ten o'clock: the stream is lively but quiet, and here and there the surface is broken by the recurring swirl of a swaying weed; but no life disturbs it, except the occasional dive of a dabchick, the movements of a watcher or watervole. Not a bird skims the surface of the water, not a fly is to be seen on it, not a sign of living creature under it. But the fresh light air is like a caress, the warm sun shines interrupted only by the occasional passage of small white clouds, the water meadows are bright with buttercups, and the woods and hedges that are on their borders are white with hawthorn blossom or lit by the candelabra of horse-chestnut flower. Birds of many sorts, most notably blackbirds, are singing, and the angler in his hour of waiting has such entertainment as seems more than imperfect man can deserve or comprehend.

Fallodon Papers, Viscount Grey of Fallodon, 1926

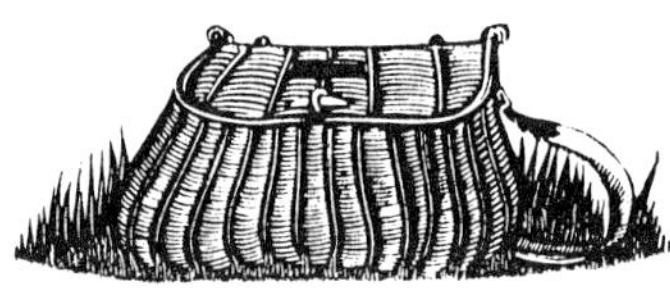

The Lightness of a Fly

Salmon fishing in very early spring is one of the most glorious forms of fly-fishing; but one of the drawbacks to it is the enormous size of the flies and weight and length of the hook that the salmon prefer at that season of the year. The sensation to the angler is that of casting the body of a small bird at the end of the line all the time. There is perceptible increase in pleasure to the angler when in May the smaller and lighter flies become more attractive to the fish than the larger ones.

The lightness of a fly makes the use of a comparatively slender and lively rod, not only possible, but an advantage in casting, and the liveliness of the rod contributes greatly to the liveliness of the fish and to the pleasure in hooking and playing it. The numbness of a stiff rod is a drawback to trolling and heavier methods of fishing.

Fallodon Papers, Viscount Grey of Fallodon, 1926

Acknowledgements

PICTURE CREDITS

Front cover: *The Fishing Party*, attributed to Joseph Farington and John Hoppner (Victoria Art Gallery, Bath)
Title page: *An Angler in a River Valley*, after A. A. Glendening (Bridgeman Art Library/Private Collection)

2 *Going North, 1893*, George Earl (Christopher Wood Ltd/National Railway Museum, York)
5 *Going to the Meet*, Sir Alfred Munnings (Laing Art Gallery, Newcastle upon Tyne/Tyne and Wear Museums Service)
6 *By the Kennels*, Wright Barker (Bridgeman/Bonhams)
7 *The Prince of Wales at Easton Neston, 1887*, Royal Archives Windsor © reserved. Reproduced by gracious permission of Her Majesty the Queen.
9 *The Fallowfield Hunt, the Hunt Breakfast at the Three Pigeons*, Cecil Aldin (Bridgeman/Private Collection)
11 *The Cheshire Hunt: the Meet at Calverley Hall*, George Goodwin Kilburne (Fine Art Photographs)
13 *A Good Day's Sport*, Edward Benjamin Herberte (Fine Art Photographs/ Anthony Mitchell Fine Paintings, Nottingham)
15 *The Cheshire Hunt: Making for Peckforton Hills*, George Goodwin Kilburne (Fine Art Photographs)
17 *Returning Home After a Hard Day*, Charles Edward Stewart (Fine Art Photographs)
19 *A Hunter and his Pack, 1870*, Edwin Frederick Holt (Fine Art Photographs)
21 *The Prince of Wales at Elveden Hall, Suffolk*, Royal Archives Windsor © reserved. Reproduced by gracious permission of Her Majesty the Queen.
23 *Pheasant Shooting in the Forest*, S.J.E. Jones (Fine Art Photographs)
25 *Pheasants, 1909*, Archibald Thorburn (Fine Art Photographs)
27 *The Hon. Sir Ailwyn Fellowes Pheasant Shoot, 1911* (Hulton Picture Company)
29 *Shooting Party at Blenhelm Palace* (courtesy His Grace the Duke of Marlborough)
31 *Partridge Shoot at Six Mile Bottom*, John F. Herring, Senior (Bridgeman/Christie's, London)
33 *Going South, 1895*, George Earl (Christopher Wood Gallery/National Railway Museum, York)
35 *Prince Albert at Balmoral, 1860*, Edwin Landseer (Royal Library Windsor © reserved. Reproduced by permission of Her Majesty the Queen)
37 *The Monarch of the Glen*, Edwin Landseer (Bridgeman/John Dewar & Sons)
39 *In the Highlands*, Archibald Thorburn (Fine Art Photographs)
41 *The Fishing Party*, attributed to Joseph Farington and John Hoppner (Victoria Art Gallery, Bath)
43 *On the River Dee*, Henry John Boddington (Fine Art Photographs/Private Collection)
45 *A Rest from Fishing*, Alexander Rolfe (Fine Art Photographs/Omell Gallery)
47 *Still Life with Salmon & Terrier*, John Russell (Fine Art Photographs)
49 *The Spiddal River*, Anon
51 *Anglers Playing Their Catch*, D. Wolstenholme (Bridgeman/Gavin Graham Gallery, London)
53 *English Landscape with Fishermen*, Anon (Bridgeman/Roy Miles Fine Paintings, London)
55 *A River Landscape*, Edward Charles Williams (Bridgeman/Private Collection)

TEXT CREDITS

Text extracts from the following sources are reprinted with the kind permission of the publishers and copyright holders stated. Should any copyright holder have been inadvertently omitted they should apply to the publishers who would be pleased to credit them in any subsequent editions.

10 Henry Williamson, *The Sun in the Sands* (Faber & Faber, 1945)
18, 20, 26, 28: J.G. Ruffer *The Big Shots* (Quiller Press, 1989)
38 Edmund Luxmoore *Deer Stalking*, (David & Charles Ltd, 1980 © Edmund Luxmoore)

First published in Great Britain 1991 by
PAVILION BOOKS LIMITED
196 Shaftesbury Avenue, London WC2H 8JL

Designed by Andrew Barron & Collis Clements Associates

A CIP catalogue record for this book is available from the British Library

ISBN 1-85145-774-7

Printed and bound in Scotland by Eagle Colour Books

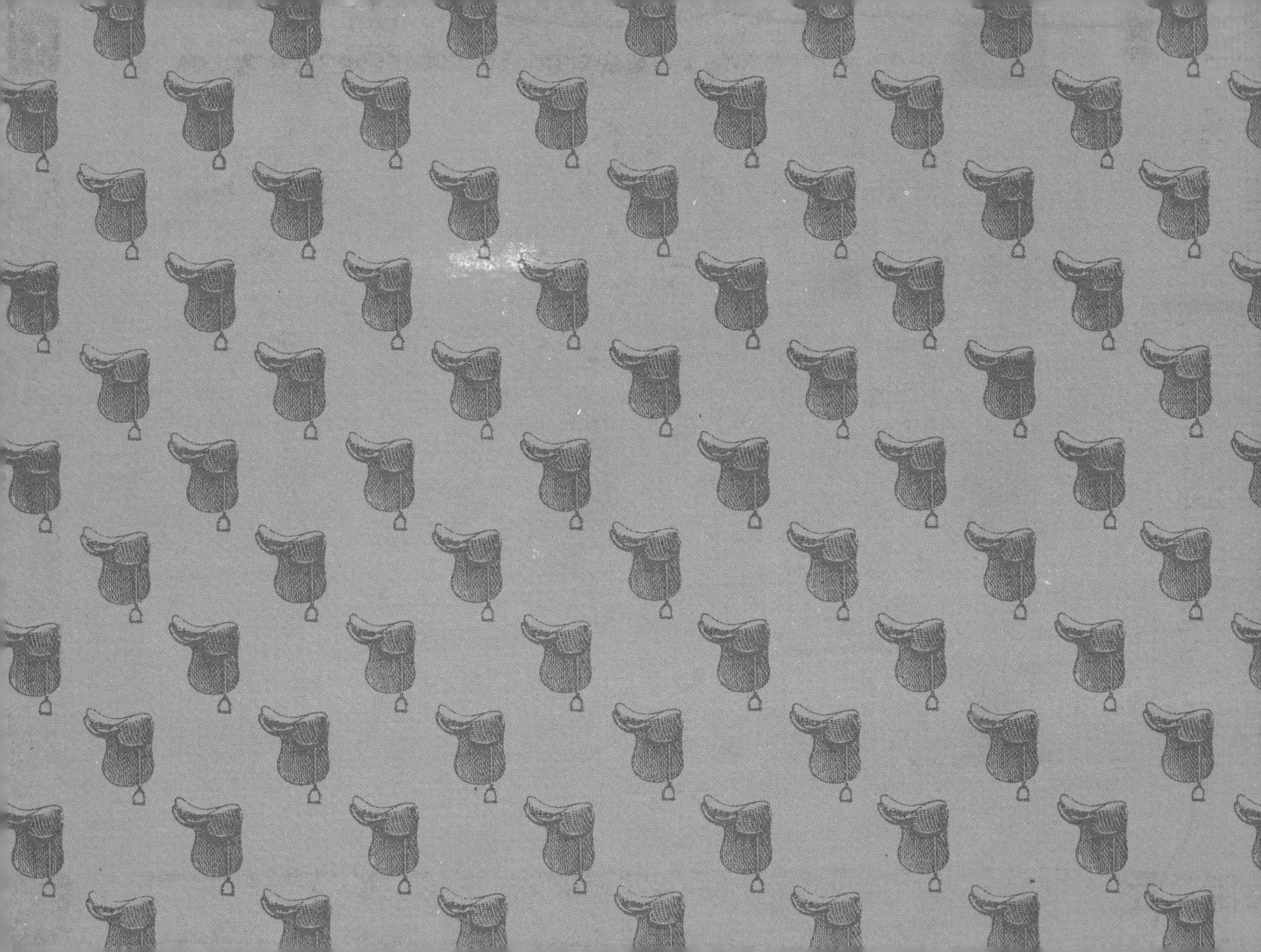